How it is made

Skyscrapers

Text   Duncan Michael
Design   Ray Carpenter

Contents

ff
faber and faber in association with Threshold Books

All kinds of skyscrapers

Skyscrapers are usually built in the centres of large cities. Their many floors, stacked one above the other, provide useful space for people to live and work in, and most of them are designed as offices for large organizations, such as banks or oil companies. Some are planned as hotels, apartment blocks or, occasionally, as a hospital, a factory, or even a warehouse. Many skyscrapers offer a mixture of accommodation – shops, offices, apartments, and car parks.

Because of the high price of land in city centres they are generally developed in clusters rather than in single units, but they are always planned so that there are spaces between each building. The most famous clusters of skyscrapers in the world are those on the island of Manhattan in New York City. An outstanding example of the practical value of high-rise buildings is in Hong Kong where the best possible use has been made of a very limited amount of space.

The basic form, or **footprint**, of a skyscraper is generally a simple square, rectangle or circle. Its eventual size, shape and appearance will depend on its situation and function. The materials and design of skyscrapers in North America will not be the same as those in Africa, for example. However, there is one common architectural feature, which is that they become smaller in plan as they reach upwards; the taller the building the more noticeable is the reduction.

Above: Chicago, home of the first skyscraper, now has the world's tallest, the Sears Tower seen in the background skyline.

Below: Hong Kong. Skyscrapers, which provide offices and homes for an ever-growing population, crowd the land between sea and mountain.

Opposite: New York. A bird's-eye photograph of Manhattan Island taken from immediately over the Pan Am Building. You can clearly see how the buildings, set-back, become smaller in plan as they grow higher.

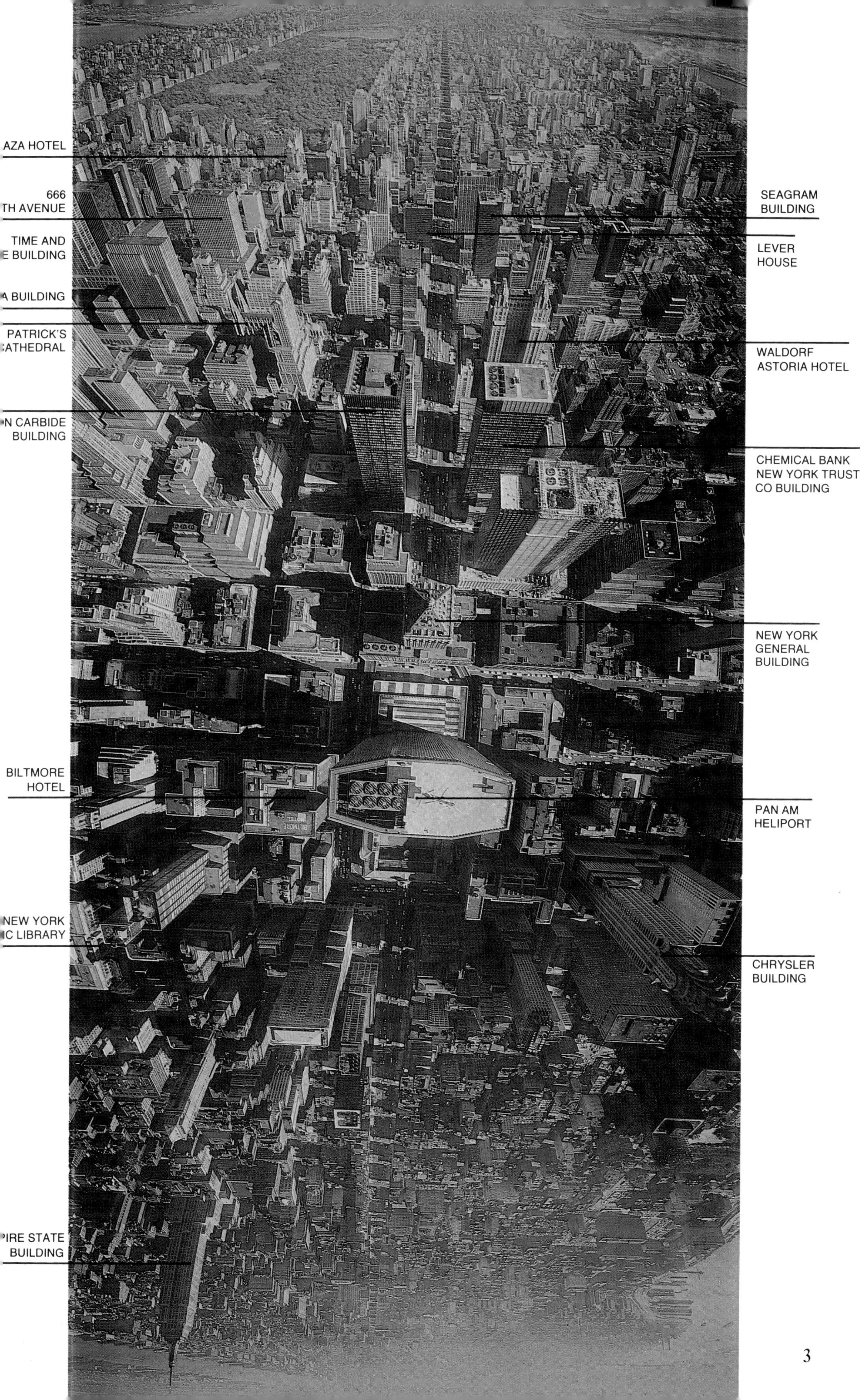

AZA HOTEL

666
TH AVENUE

TIME AND
E BUILDING

A BUILDING

PATRICK'S
CATHEDRAL

N CARBIDE
BUILDING

BILTMORE
HOTEL

NEW YORK
C LIBRARY

IRE STATE
BUILDING

SEAGRAM
BUILDING

LEVER
HOUSE

WALDORF
ASTORIA HOTEL

CHEMICAL BANK
NEW YORK TRUST
CO BUILDING

NEW YORK
GENERAL
BUILDING

PAN AM
HELIPORT

CHRYSLER
BUILDING

3

What is a skyscraper?

Tall structures are the most spectacular and famous man-made landmarks in the world, from the Great Pyramid of Cheops in Egypt to the Empire State Building in New York, from the temple of Borobodur in Indonesia to the Eiffel Tower in Paris. Lighthouses, clock towers, monuments, steeples, minarets, television towers – all are designed to reach towards the sky. But as well as having the power to attract attention and to excite those who look up at them, tall buildings also have an important practical value, which has been realized by builders throughout the centuries. Even in nature the advantage of high-rise building is utilized – by termites. In some areas of the world their columns of mud can reach over 9 metres (29 feet) high. Their structure solves many of the same problems as those experienced by the builders of skyscrapers.

In the Middle Ages, castles and keeps were tall, as well as massive. They were generally built on high ground, to increase their defensive capability. The builders of the great mediaeval cathedrals made use of height in their desire to glorify God and acknowledge the importance of the Church.

In the Twentieth Century this same urge to build upwards, driven by the practical need to make the best use of space, has found expression in skyscrapers, and the results can be equally exciting. There is no more spectacular sight than that of the New York and Hong Kong skylines at night when the lights in the buildings contrast with the darkness high up in the sky, and are reflected in the waters far below.

The ambitions of the owners of the skyscrapers and even the cities in which they are built also play their part. There always seems to be an urge to build higher and higher. At present, Chicago – where the first skyscraper was built – claims the world's tallest building. It is the headquarters of Sears Roebuck, a giant shopping chain, and has 110 storeys reaching a height of 443 metres (1454 feet).

Now that skyscrapers have reached such spectacular heights, there is only marginal visual advantage in going even higher. The eye just cannot tell the difference. Nonetheless, plans for even taller buildings are always being conceived and developed. In 1957, Frank Lloyd Wright, one of the most famous of all American architects, proposed a 'mile high' building. Plans under present consideration are for the Television City complex in New York City which will be 509 metres (1670 feet) high, the Schrique Project in Phoenix, Arizona, 515 metres (1692 feet), and a 614-metre (2015 feet) building in Atlanta, Georgia. All these buildings bid to be the world's tallest. In contrast the tallest skyscraper in Britain, proposed for Canary Wharf in London, will be 260 metres (850 feet).

Top left: Nature invented the skyscraper. For thousands of years termites have built mud tower-blocks to live in and to defend themselves from attack. Inside the towers they have solved many of the problems of organization which have to be considered in the designing of skyscrapers.

Top centre: In some of the ancient cities of the world, tenement houses, crowded close together, were built as high as ten storeys. A spectacular example of this traditional architecture can be seen in Sana'a, the capital of Yemen. Made from mud bricks, the buildings are painted and decorated with Arab patterns. They even have shafts running up them, taking fresh air to each level.

Top right: The spire of Salisbury Cathedral, 123m (404ft) high, shown here in a painting by John Constable, dominates the town around it, where most of the buildings are only two or three storeys high. Completed in 1265, this was the tallest building in Britain for over 600 years.

Bottom left: Though not strictly a skyscraper, the Eiffel Tower, at 300m (986ft), is one of the world's most famous tall buildings. Every year hundreds of thousands of tourists climb to its top to see the magnificent views of Paris. It was built in 1889 for an exhibition to celebrate French technical achievements.

Bottom centre: The Sears Tower in Chicago is currently the world's tallest building. The external cladding is mainly glass; in the photograph you can see how this acts like a mirror, reflecting the sky.

Bottom right: This photograph, taken in 1957, shows Frank Lloyd Wright giving a lecture about his ideas for a 'mile high' building. Such a skyscraper, over three times taller than the Sears Tower, could be built, but it would present very difficult problems for the architect, the engineer and the builder.

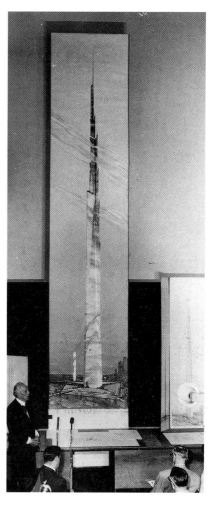

Planning and design

A great deal of discussion and planning obviously has to take place before the building work can start. To begin with, an organization – or in some cases an individual – has to be prepared to provide the huge sums of money that will be needed. Next, a suitable site has to be found. Then the architects and the engineers have to be chosen. Though they work closely together, and though each is influenced by the ideas of the other, basically they have separate functions. The architect's reponsibility is to plan the building, so that it satisfies the needs of the owner as well as fitting into the city scene. He will be concerned with the shape of the building and the materials used for cladding it, while the engineer tackles the more technical problems – the strength, the size, the machinery.

First, rough sketches of the basic ideas are produced. Then more detailed drawings are prepared, and gradually a definite design emerges. As modern skyscrapers are so complex and sophisticated, many different specialists in architecture and engineering are involved. Their design and planning problems are never straightforward. Unexpected difficulties often arise, and the designers may have to change their ideas many times before the final plans can be completed. When problems are particularly complicated, special research has to be carried out. For example, the wind pressures on the faces of a building are often difficult to predict, and to obtain the necessary information a scale model of the proposed building and site are made. This is put in a wind tunnel, where all parts of the faces of the building are tested in every possible wind direction. Nowadays, computers are used for analysing the resulting data – as they are for many other functions, such as forecasting the way that the building will sway in the wind, for making perspective drawings and construction plans, and for quantifying various components.

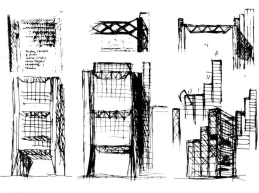

FIRST STAGE · VARIATIONS ON COMPETITION SCHEME · 1979

SECOND VERSION · INCLINED SUSPENSION STRUCTURE · 1980·

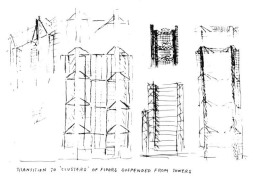

TRANSITION TO 'CLUSTERS' OF FLOORS SUSPENDED FROM TOWERS

Norman Foster's sketches showing the development of the concept design of the Hongkong and Shanghai Banking Corporation headquarters.

Cross-section through the final building showing the set-backs as the skyscraper gets higher. The tunnel brings in sea-water for cooling the building.

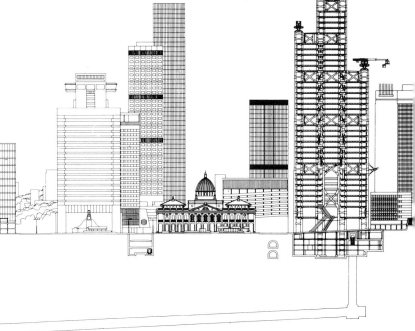

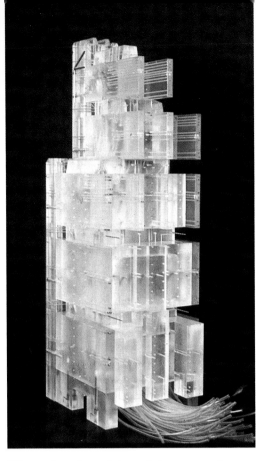

The engineer's model, made in perspex, has small tubes leading to each part of the elevation so that the air pressure can be measured.

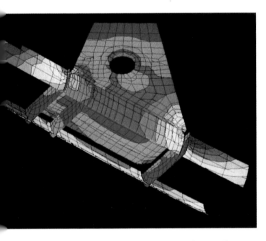

Using a computer, the engineer analyses the stresses in all parts of the structure. These can be shown in picture form to help develop the design. Each colour in this picture of a structural joint represents a different value of stress.

As there were not adequate records of wind conditions in Hong Kong, a model of the whole city was built. This was placed in a giant wind tunnel so that the buildings could be tested in winds of different speeds and direction.

Other natural forces, such as earthquakes, can shake a skyscraper at its base. The vibrations have to be absorbed by the building, but fortunately they take time to travel up a skyscraper, so this problem is not as serious for the engineer as one might imagine.

Very rarely are two skyscrapers identical: their use, the site, the time available, and the people, all vary. But there are 'families' of buildings, which have a recognizable style developed by particular architects who have influenced each other. The first generation of skyscrapers (which were only 10 to 12 storeys high) were developed as far back as the 1890s in Chicago, and in St Louis, Missouri, from the designs of Louis Sullivan.

A significant year in the design and planning of skyscrapers was 1916, when New York City introduced laws requiring buildings to have **set-backs** related to their height. This was to ensure that the buildings would have adequate light and ventilation. Three years earlier, the architects of the Woolworth Building, 242 metres (792 feet) high, had foreseen and had made allowances for this problem, and their example was followed for the Empire State, 381 metres (1250 feet), and the Chrysler building.

The art déco skyscrapers of the 1930s were often elaborately decorated, or **clad**, in natural materials such as stone. In the 1950s a dramatic change took place with the starkly dramatic glass towers designed by Mies van der Rohe. Buildings of this kind, such as the Seagram Building in New York (1959), influenced architects throughout the world. In recent years there has been a totally different concept in design, with the work of Michael Graves, Helmut Jahn and Kohn Pedersen Fox, which uses form and decoration together, instead of treating them separately.

Unlike cars, aeroplanes, or even ships, skyscrapers cannot be bought as production models with optional extras. Each building is unique, though the designers use as many standard components as they can. A problem for the purchaser is that he will not be able to see what he is buying until it is completed. It is vital, therefore, for him to be involved at every stage of the design process. As the scheme develops he can then ask for adjustments to be made where necessary.

How construction is organized

When the design of the skyscraper is more or less complete, the purchaser, who has by now approved the plans and models of his building – is anxious for the project to go ahead. So, without delay, the builder is chosen, the production programme and price are agreed, and the work begins.

The builder's aim is to carry out the construction as efficiently as he can, and to produce a result which will match up to the purchaser's expectations, in the time specified by the contract. However, the builder's major problem is that he can only carry out the construction work one stage at a time. Also, there is a limit to the number of men and the amount of equipment that can be usefully deployed on the site.

To alleviate this problem, many of the components of the skyscraper are pre-fabricated in small workshops or large factories in various parts of the world. They are then transported to the site, and assembled on the spot.

Anyone who has watched a tall building being constructed will know that the most spectacular item of equipment is the crane. These wonderfully manoeuvrable vehicles are used for lifting into position all the components and materials. As the skyscraper grows upwards the cranes are fixed to it so that they can operate up to the highest part.

To enable workers to reach all levels of the construction safely and quickly, hoists or temporary lifts, are fixed to the outside of the building.

Enormous quantities of concrete are needed, and specially designed pumps are used for pumping it in liquid form through large diameter pipes which can reach even the most inaccessible parts of the building.

When all the components have been assembled and fitted, and each stage has been completed, the building has to be commissioned. This means that all the operating parts

This photograph, taken in the 1920s, shows workmen riding on the hook of a crane. Nowadays this dangerous practice is illegal.

The modern workman doesn't take risks. His safety harness holds him to the steelwork, and his helmet protects his head from falling objects.

This construction photograph of the National Westminster Bank in London shows much of the equipment used in building a skyscraper. The central concrete core is under construction by the slip-form method. As it goes higher, the cranes climb with it. The building is surrounded with scaffolding which provides access for the workmen as they fix the external cladding. Enormous cranes lift the steel and concrete beams, modules, etc. The builders have to be very organized, as there is very little space in which to work.

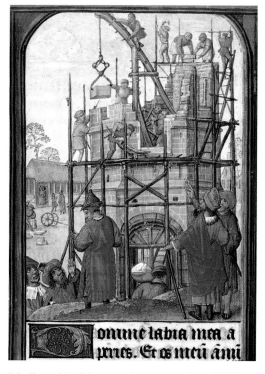

Mediaeval builders used cranes and scaffolding which very closely resemble modern methods. Compare this picture with that of the National Westminster Bank.

The construction of skyscrapers requires very brave and skilful men, as shown in this picture, taken high above New York City.

– elevators, windows, lighting, ventilation, telephones, drains – have to be tested, balanced and tuned. The building will then be ready for occupation.

Looking at a skyscraper during its construction you may wonder how it can ever be successfully completed. Also, apart from the cranes up in the sky and the earth-moving equipment below, there doesn't seem to be much going on. But hidden away there are literally hundreds of men working at dozens of different jobs. A great project creates its own team spirit, and as completion day draws nearer, the pressure and the excitement grow.

Foundations

To accommodate this huge weight on the individual columns, the foundations of a skyscraper must be carefully designed and constructed. As well as being strong enough, they have to settle in a relatively balanced and even way. If there is more than the slightest distortion, the skyscraper's lifts, cladding and partitions will be adversely affected.

The ground under the site may be of hard rock; of soft, loose soil; or, more often, it will be in layers of different substances. If the rock can easily be reached, the engineer will design the foundations to make use of it. They may have to be dug down a long way until he is happy that it is sound. Digging in rock is relatively easy.

To carry the skyscraper's weight through any softer layers, **piles** will be used. These are concrete or steel columns hammered into the ground until they penetrate the hard layer. Or they can be made by drilling shafts in the ground and filling them with fresh concrete. These are just two of many efficient piling techniques which have been developed.

If the strong soil lies too deep, the engineer can devize foundations by laying a thick raft of concrete right across the site, thus spreading the load as widely as possible over the weak soil. Another way is to 'float' the building by excavating a very deep basement, so that the weight of the skyscraper is only a little more than the weight of the materials which have been removed. The engineer may use a combination of these methods to achieve the safest, fastest and cheapest foundation.

To provide more space, basements are generally built under skyscrapers. They are expensive and take time to build, but as well as being useful they form a practical part of the structure. After the piles have been sunk, to speed up the work the builder may begin by constructing the first floor, and then have two gangs, one erecting the skyscraper upwards and the other mining its way down below to build the basements.

With city pavements or neighbours on all four sides, it is impossible to avoid an amount of disturbance when building something as big as a skyscraper. All materials move, even rock, when the loads on them change. During excavation, the ground around the building will move inwards, and water pumped from the excavation will allow the ground to settle. These movements, added to the settlement caused by the weight of the skyscraper, form a 'dish of settlement', which is greatest at the centre of the building and extends well beyond the site boundaries. If the soil is weak or the basement excavation has to be deep, a containment wall can be made by excavating a very deep trench and filling it with concrete. This is known as a diaphragm wall. While it is being dug, the trench is held

The type of foundation depends upon the depth of ground strong enough to support the weight of the building. Where the ground is soft, piles must be driven deep. If rock is near the surface, the foundations can sit directly on it.

Piles are columns of concrete or steel, driven or 'formed' in the ground. This photograph shows a steel pile being driven into the earth by a very heavy hammer which is lifted by the crane and dropped on to the pile.

open by keeping it full of a special thin, soft mud. Certain individual engineers and organizations specialize in foundation techniques, assisting the various builders on their sites. This is one of the ways in which the technology of construction is able to progress.

A collapsed street, a burst water main, or a split in a neighbour's wall are bad news, but they can happen with no obvious warning. So the movements of selected points in the soil around the site are carefully and accurately measured by surveyors throughout the construction programme. Other data such as water levels and movements at existing cracks are also logged. With the help of this information the engineers can check whether their forecasts are proving to be accurate. If the measurements indicate a growing problem connected with soil or water or neighbouring buildings, it is not at all easy to change plans, but at least any problems of serious damage can be avoided.

A diaphragm wall is formed by cutting a narrow trench deep into the ground. Here the steel is in position just before the concrete is placed.

Piles can be formed by drilling a hole into the ground and filling it with concrete.

The position of the structure has to be accurately checked.

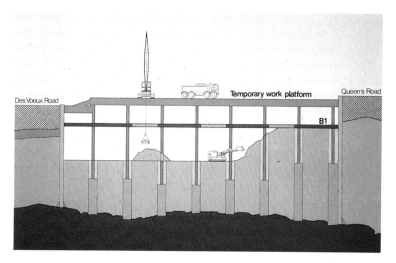

The piles have been driven down to firm ground, and a diaphragm wall has been built around the site. As the basement is excavated the slabs are cast and then the ground is dug from under them.

Steel structures

The **self-weight** of a skyscraper is around 100,000 tonnes. Added to this is the (relatively insignificant) weight of its occupants and their equipment. The structure which is needed to bear all this weight must be very strong and safe. For example, if built wrongly, a skyscraper could collapse by crumbling under its own weight; or – more likely – it could start wobbling and then buckle as it loses stability. The steel frame, developed nearly a hundred years ago, consists of long pieces of steel which are assembled into beams and columns to form a three-dimensional skeleton for the building. The floor decks – usually made of thin slabs of concrete moulded on corrugated metal sheets – are fitted on to the beams at each level. Though by no means ideal, steel is still the best structural material that we have, to date.

The various parts of the frame are designed in the required shapes, sizes and thicknesses by the structural engineer, and are prefabricated at specialist workshops from steel provided by the rolling mills. The steelwork pieces are produced so that they will be manageable for the particular crane which will be used, and are assembled and fitted on the site.

Typical shapes of rolled steel members used in construction.

Riveters working at the top of a skyscraper in New York. In the background is the Chrysler Building.

In the past, the pieces of steelwork forming the frame were joined up by **rivets**. Nowadays, they are bolted or welded. **Welding** provides a very neat and strong joint, but to be successful it must be carried out by skilled operators.

This welder is using a system known as electric arc welding. An electric current heats up the steel that is to be welded. The welder wears a mask and visor to protect his eyes from the intense glare.

A skyscraper always sways around in the wind – it may experience a force which can be as much as 2000 tonnes acting over the face of the building. The occupants will not notice movements of up to half a metre (18 inches) because at the top of the building there is nothing to relate them to. They may, however, feel a little uncomfortable. To ensure that as much as possible of the weight of the structure counteracts the wind, the designers arrange the outer members accordingly – with diagonal bracing on the face of the building, or a tapered vertical profile, or heavy beams right across and around the buildings. All these are made of steel.

A very wide, clear floor area near the base of the skyscraper may be needed, in which case most of the **columns** have to be omitted. Many different structural patterns have been used to reduce the number of columns – some of them very dramatic, such as stiffening the **façade** with diagonals or large beams, or using an **umbrella frame** high up in the building and suspending the columns so that they act as **hangers** for carrying the floors.

Because steel is so strong, the thickness of each piece is typically about 30 mm ($1\frac{1}{4}$ inches). But in a fire, steel can

The diagonal steel bracing on the John Hancock Building, Chicago, stiffens the structure against wind loads.

The engineer has a choice of methods by which the separate pieces of steel can be joined, to form the structural frame. Before he can advance the design he has to consider the weight of the building, the wind loads, the shape of the site, the use of the building, and the problems of construction.

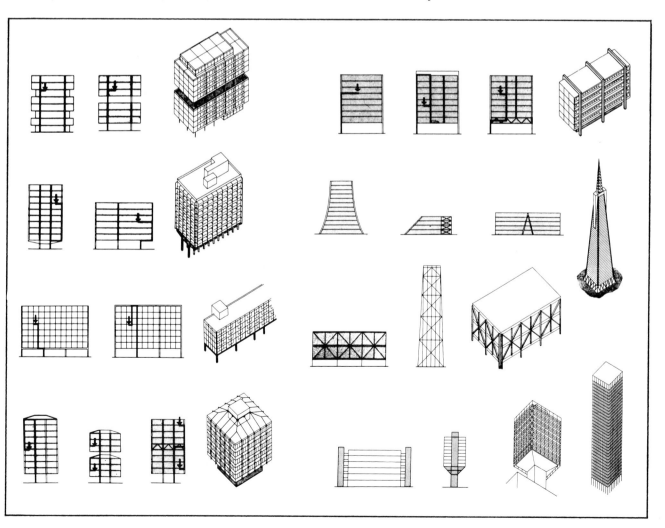

heat up very quickly, and without protection it can reach temperatures of about 1000°C (2120°F). At this point the metal has little strength or elasticity, and it expands considerably. To prevent such a potential hazard the important parts of the frames are covered with **insulating jackets**. Originally these were made of concrete but today **lightweight fibre**, plaster or **vermiculite** are more commonly used. Another method of fire prevention is for the steel to be in tube form. The tubes are filled with water connected to a storage tank which continually keeps the water flowing inside the tubes so that it will cool the steel if there should be a fire.

Great care is always taken to ensure that in case of fire, safe ways are provided for people to escape and for firemen to be able to carry out their job quickly and effectively. Staircases are specially protected, and lifts and equipment are provided so that the firemen can take their hoses high up the building.

The Seagram Building, designed by Mies van der Rohe, is considered to be the most significant building of the Modern Movement. Its clean, stark lines, and the richness of the bronze and glass finish, have been copied, but not equalled, throughout the world.

Right: This photograph of the Hongkong and Shanghai Bank shows all the stages of forming the protection of the steelwork columns. To prevent corrosion, the columns (before they were erected) were sprayed with a special concrete. After they had been welded together, the joints were treated with the same material. The columns were then wrapped in an insulating jacket which was protected with aluminium foil. All of this protection was then covered with aluminium cladding made in St Louis, USA.

Opposite: The Citicorp Center was designed to give as much free space at ground level as possible, allowing an existing church to be rebuilt on the site. The weight of the building is 'collected' by the huge beams around the base of the tower and then taken to the ground by four large columns on the middle of each face. The cladding is like a tight skin wrapped around the building. You can compare this picture with the front cover, which shows the building under construction.

14

Concrete structures

Concrete is a mixture of small, strong stones, cement and water which has been densely compacted and left to mature. It is very strong in **compression** and is durable. As it cracks when stretched, it is designed to contain bars of embedded steel. This reinforced concrete is the most versatile and cheapest structural material available. It is even more effective if the steel reinforcement in the concrete is tightened up, or **pre-stressed**.

The concrete frame is made by pouring the wet mixture into moulds and leaving it to harden. If the process is carried out in a factory the concrete is called precast. If the moulds are used on the site it is called insitu concrete. The joints between the pieces of concrete can be very neatly made, and an infinite variety of moulded shapes becomes available.

Concrete can be made with **porous aggregates** which weigh much less than ordinary concrete but which are still strong. This material is used where the ground cannot carry much extra new load as in the One Shell Plaza in Houston, Texas, which is 218 metres (715 feet) tall. It weighs only three quarters of the weight it would have been if built from ordinary concrete.

For skyscrapers over the height of 200 metres (650 feet), steelwork is the cheapest method of construction. Below that height, it is design requirements which determine the choice of structural material. Steelwork and reinforced concrete can be used for different parts of the same skyscraper. They can even be used together for individual items. For buildings with a large number of dividing walls, such as hotels, the walls themselves, when made of re-inforced concrete, act as the load-bearing structure. With efficiently designed mould systems they can be quickly built, work on the next storey beginning immediately after the concrete has set. In another system known as **slip forming** the moulds are continuously drawn up in very small steps while the mixed concrete is in the process of setting. Slip forming is used when lift-shafts and stair-wells in the centre of an office block are to be made from concrete; also for tall chimneys and concrete oil production platforms.

In a concrete skyscraper the floors can be made from solid, flat slabs, leaving more headroom for the pipework and airducts. For this work, insitu concrete is generally used, but sometimes the lift slab method – in which whole floors are hoisted into place – is preferred.

An outstanding example of a concrete skyscraper is the Standard Bank headquarters in Johannesburg, South Africa. Built in the mid-1960s, its form reflects the exciting architectural and construction ideas which were being explored at that time. It consists of three sets of ten floors,

Only a few weeks separate these two photographs. By using the lift slab method, the builder casts the concrete slabs on top of each other, rather like a pack of cards. Special jacks, on the same principle as those used for a car with a flat tyre, lift the slabs up the columns. When the slabs are at their correct level they are then joined to the columns with insitu concrete.

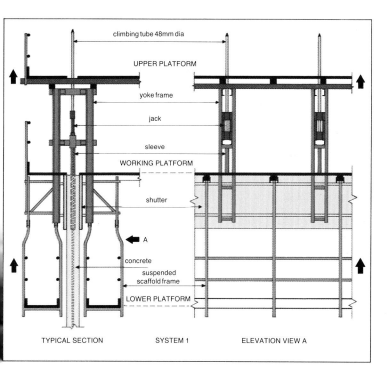

TYPICAL SECTION   SYSTEM 1   ELEVATION VIEW A

This diagram shows the equipment used to slip-form concrete. The shutters or formwork are fixed to a very strong steel frame called the 'yoke'. To this yoke is fixed the climbing jack which grips a vertical tube. As the concrete is poured into the shutter from the working platform, the jack climbs up the tube a few millimetres at a time, and pulls the whole apparatus with it.

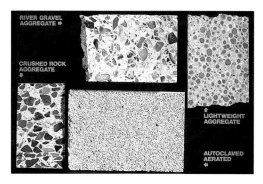

Concrete is made from many different types of aggregate. This photograph shows cut-through sections of some of them.

Left and below: These photographs show the sequence of casting concrete walls using the slip form method. The first photograph shows the jack fixed in the yoke before the climbing tube is in position. In the next, the whole frame is ready to lift when the reinforcement has been fixed. The last shows the top of the wall after the concrete has been poured.

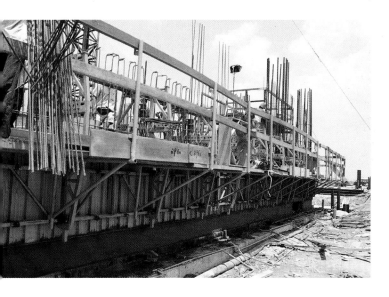

17

Above, left to right: After demolition of the old buildings on the site, a pit was dug to the lowest basement level where the four foundation piers for the skyscraper were excavated to sound rock. Then the square central core structure was made in reinforced concrete by the slip form technique. By the time that the first set of giant pre-stressed concrete cantilevers had been made, many of the lightweight concrete floor beams and the hangers had been precast in a factory outside the city. These were laid out at the site on huge steel trays which were then hauled up into position, a quarter floor at a time. For this bold construction method a special rotating crane was designed and assembled on top of the core. It could lift 70 tons at a radius of 30 metres (100 feet).

In the Oversea Chinese Banking Corporation building in Singapore, slip formed concrete towers bear three sets of huge beams on which the floors are supported.

18

Above, left to right: The large cantilever beams form an umbrella frame from which the hangers support the floors underneath. With the benefit of this equipment, construction proceeded very quickly at three distinct levels, assembling the building downwards. As the tower was being formed, the basements were being fully excavated, and their walls and floors formed in reinforced concrete. Completion above and below ground was almost simultaneous. The concrete was designed and made with great care so that it would be suitable to form the cladding. This can be seen by comparing the last two photographs.

A close-up of the special crane built at the top of the core tower to lift the floor slabs into position.

each set hanging down from the central lift and service core. In this form of construction the tower block creates minimum interference with the public square at street level or with the banking hall below the square. Lower down still, there are four more basements beneath the whole of the square – enclosing vaults, plant and car parking space.

For the Broadgate development in the City of London, the cladding was made in large panels in a factory away from the site. They consisted of an aluminium frame containing the glazing and panels of polished pink granite. The large tower cranes lifted them directly into place.

These two buildings show the very different ways in which architects can design cladding. On the left is the World Trade Center in New York, designed by Minoru Yamasaki. The cladding is a screen of closely spaced vertical aluminium piers similar to the gothic styling on early skyscrapers such as the Woolworth Building, which can be seen in the background. At the Century City Center, Los Angeles, Daniel Mann Johnson Mendenhall used stainless steel and glass to provide a much lighter, highly reflective surface.

Opposite: 333 Wacker Drive, Chicago, designed by Kohn Pederson Fox, shows the magical quality that cladding can give to a building. Here the huge curved glass wall reflects the surrounding city and sky, yet through it shine the lights of the building.

Cladding the exterior

The basic purpose of cladding is to protect the building from heat and cold, to keep it dry, to cut off the wind, and to prevent the dirt and noise of the city from reaching the inhabitants. But all this must be achieved within limits. Everyone likes some natural light and views to look out on. Fresh air and entrances and exits are also essential. In buildings constructed of traditional masonry all these cladding functions and the load bearing structure were provided together. In a modern skyscraper it is more practical to treat the cladding and the structure as separate elements.

As cladding also determines the appearance of the building, it is of great significance to the owner, the architect and the public. Skyscrapers create an impression not only through their height and proportions but also through their general appearance – the texture, pattern and colour that cladding provides. At first it presented an appearance similar to that on traditional buildings. Gradually it became more and more plain, until some buildings were covered in apparently almost seamless skins of glass. Now the fashion has changed again, and many designers are using highly decorated cladding styles for skyscrapers.

To last a long time, cladding must be made of durable, fireproof materials which will continue to look good in spite of the weather. Glass has always been a good cladding material for skyscrapers. It can be made in large, smooth pieces of very uniform texture and colour; it looks clean and sleek; and it reflects the changing sky. Various metals are also used for cladding, including bronze, aluminium and stainless or painted steel. For many years, stone was regarded by architects as old-fashioned, but now granite is used in many skyscrapers, cut in very thin sheets and highly polished. Brickwork, plastics and mosaics have also been used in the cladding of skyscrapers.

Cladding does not support itself; its weight is carried by the frame, whereas with aeroplanes, ships and even cars, the outer shell is the basic structure. As it has to cover such huge areas and has to be produced to very accurate dimensions, cladding is manufactured in factories and brought on site to be assembled. It follows the frame up the building, thus permitting the fitting out of the lower floors to begin while the structure above is being built. The materials for the skeleton frame and the cladding do not have to be the same. A stone clad building need not have a concrete frame, nor need a steel and glass cladding be fixed only on a steel frame.

Equipping the interior

Once the structure has been built and the cladding fixed, a great variety of machines, appliances and fittings have to be put in place before the skyscraper can be inhabited.

Lifts, or elevators, to carry people from the ground to the floors above, are of primary importance. They must be smooth-running and swift. In some large skyscrapers they operate like a train system, with stopping slow lifts, express lifts to the top, interchange lobbies, and so on. Some of them run up the outside of the building or up through the central lobby; these have to move more slowly, but people enjoy them. Some skyscrapers have escalators on their lower floors.

Although as much use as possible is made of natural light, artificial lighting is needed throughout the various floors, as well as in lobbies, toilets and stairways. In such big buildings, the many lights, the sun, the large numbers of people, and the various machines and appliances, together generate a great deal of heat, so it is vitally important to keep the interior cool and clean. This is provided by the air-conditioning system, a very expensive item which consists of refrigerators, air cleaners and a mass of pipes or ducts throughout the building. Even in winter, little heating is required, except near windows and entrance doors, and although boilers are supplied they are principally used to provide hot water for washing and cleaning.

Not so long ago telecommunications meant telephones and switchboards, but today telex and facsimile lines plus radio and television links have to be provided. Electronic systems and computers are also used for creating what is known as **intelligent buildings**. Environmental conditions in all areas of the building are regularly measured and automatically reported to a central information base. This is programmed to analyze the data and, if discomfort is found in the conditions of some rooms, to correct it. In a large skyscraper this is a huge task, especially since conditions change all the time, and a satisfactory adjustment in one area can seriously unbalance another. Electronic monitoring systems are used for checking all the other operations in the building – such as the power supplies, the elevators and the fire alarms – and give early warnings should a fault develop. These systems are very complex and have to be regularly maintained and tuned by specialist engineers.

Modern skyscrapers often have an enormous entrance lobby or 'atrium' which is the social centre of the building and can be made very attractive with tropical shrubs and flowers, glass elevators, escalators, restaurants, shops and fountains.

As with the exterior structure, the interior of a skyscraper must also be designed to resist any possibility of fire. Non-flammable materials are used, smoke detectors are

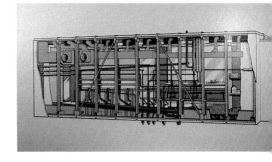

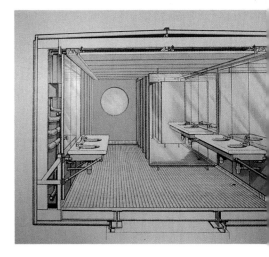

The modules, when they were delivered, were complete, both internally and externally. After they were placed, all that remained was to connect them to the water supply, the drainage and the electrical and airconditioning systems.

fixed throughout the building, water sprinklers are built into ceilings, and stairs are enclosed in extra resistant walls. With these precautions any fire which starts can easily be brought under control and then extinguished.

For so many people there must be plenty of toilets at each floor level. These are stacked vertically above each other so that all the waste pipes can run straight down and out to the sewers.

In the control room the security staff can monitor the entire performance of the building. The overhead screens are from remotely controlled television cameras at the building entrances. Those on the desks give continuous information on the performance of the machinery. The wall panels indicate any faults in the various electrical and alarm systems.

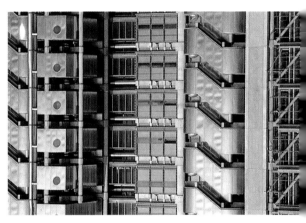

To achieve the highest possible quality of manufacture and to ensure rapid erection, the toilet units or modules for the new Lloyd's building in the City of London were made in a factory, brought to the site on a lorry, and lifted by crane into position.

Left: In very large buildings, natural daylight cannot always be enjoyed by all the occupants. Architects have tried to overcome this problem by adopting the old Roman concept of an atrium, or light well, in the middle of the building. Atria provide dramatic open spaces, such as this one in the State of Illinois Building, Chicago (designed by Helmut Jahn) which is over 16 storeys high. Here glass-sided lifts climb between the floors, giving passengers exciting views of the interior of the building.

Servicing a skyscraper

Once the skyscraper is occupied, operating it is a never-ending business, and all the many activities have to be taken into consideration when it is being designed. Each day, huge quantities of mail arrive and leave. Within the building, messengers carry documents from floor to floor. Food and drinks are brought in. The mass of rubbish which accumulates each day has to be bundled up in the basement and then trucked out. Every evening, staff arrive to wash and clean the interior of the building.

Quite frequently, lifts have to be reset because the **ropes** stretch; telephones have to be moved; lights have to be adjusted or changed. So maintenance men are always in the building.

The polluted atmosphere in a city is very damaging to all materials, so the exterior has to be regularly inspected, and necessary repairs or cleaning carried out. The windows and glass cladding must also be cleaned. All this work is done by men moving about the façade in **cradles** which are operated by cranes on the roof.

Good quality construction work is very difficult and disruptive to carry out after the skyscraper is completed and occupied. The materials and construction methods are devized to give as long a life as possible without having to be repaired, especially on the exterior. Some present-day materials have not yet been put to the test of time. The internal equipment – chillers, lifts, electronic controls – will not last as long as the building. Certain items may become worn out or just obsolete. In all skyscrapers, every ten or so years, major parts have to be taken out and replaced.

The occupants of the building also change – either because a company decides to reorganize itself, or because it leaves the building altogether. As long as the structure is not affected, whole floors can be cleared of all their walls and furniture and laid out in a quite different way to suit the new occupants. So even if the perfect skyscraper could be built, of perfect materials all perfectly assembled, its interior would undergo complete changes.

So that this huge crane could lift a replacement aerial to a height of 120 metres (400 feet) on the Telecom Tower in London, it was necessary to close all the surrounding roads.

Because of the continual advances in modern technology, such as in satellite communications, new equipment has to be fitted on to existing buildings.

Opposite: To enable men to work on the face of a skyscraper, cranes are provided for lowering the cradles. The cranes are permanently fixed to the building.

Stage by stage

The amount of man hours, money and materials involved in the making of a skyscraper is enormous. As an example, the following is a list of key dates in the building of the Hongkong and Shanghai Bank head office in Hong Kong.

Spring 1978   The idea of constructing a new headquarters to fulfil future needs was first discussed by the Directors of the Bank.

January 1979   The Bank appointed a team of engineers and architects to examine the feasibility of making a new building within the existing headquarters site, as it did not want to move away if this could be avoided.

March 1979   A number of ways in which a new building could be achieved were described in the report of the study team. The Bank decided to create a building which would be 'the finest in the world'.

June 1979   An ideas competition was run by the Bank. Seven distinguished architects – two each from Australia, the United Kingdom and the USA, and one from Hong Kong – were invited to take part.

November 1979   The Bank selected the British architects, Foster Associates, from the seven competitors. The design team was assembled, with Ove Arup & Partners as the structural engineers and J Roger Preston as the building services engineers.

May 1980   The development of earlier ideas was presented by the designers to the Bank.

October 1980   Testing of models for wind effects on the building and the surrounding areas was started at the University of Western Ontario.

October 1980   So that there could be an early start on site, a contractor, John Lok Wimpey, was appointed to manage the construction.

December 1980   The final concept design was presented to the Bank for approval, proceeding to detailed design for construction.

June 1981   Once the bank workers had moved out to temporary offices in the city, demolition of the old building was started.

September 1981   The makers of the cladding, Cupples of St Louis, Missouri, were appointed. This allowed the time which would be needed to develop components and make them.

October 1981   The firm to construct and erect the structural steel frame of the building was selected, British Steel Corporation/Dorman Long from the United Kingdom.

November 1981   The construction of the basement diaphragm walls by Bachy Soletanche from France started on site.

December 1981   The toilets and equipment rooms were to be fabricated in a factory and shipped to site complete. HMT Consort from Japan were chosen for this package.

June 1982   Excavations of hand-dug shafts began on site. The building foundations were to be formed at the bottom of all these shafts.

January 1983   The steelwork, which had been shipped to Hong Kong and fire-protected, began to arrive on site for erection. Excavations under the street level floor continued downwards to create the basements.

November 1983   The first toilet and service modules arrived at the site for installation on the steel frame.

January 1984   Fixing of the cladding to the steel frame began on site.

May 1984   The basement structure was completed.

October 1984   The steel frame was completed while the cladding, machinery, air conditioning, lifts, escalators, floors, ceilings and services continued to be installed.

July 1985   The banking hall and the lower floors of the building were taken over by the Bank and re-opened for business.

November 1985   The Bank took over the rest of the building for occupation.

During the construction of the Hongkong and Shanghai Bank over 5000 people were employed on the site, coming from 15 different organizations from countries as far away as Great Britain, United States, France, Germany, as well as Hong Kong itself. Materials and components came from all over the world – Great Britain, United States, Japan, Italy, Germany – by sea and air.

The old traditional method of bamboo scaffolding was also used in conjunction with modern methods of construction.

Who creates a skyscraper?

THE CITY
who check and approve

- Town plan match
- Correct building construction
- Supply of electricity, water, telephones, gas, drains
- Road traffic
- Fire protection
  and so on

THE OWNER
who organises

- The provider of money
- The financial advisor
- The letting agent
- The occupiers
  and so on

THE ARCHITECT
who organises

- The planner
- The structural engineer
- The mechanical engineer
- The electrical engineer
- The geotechnical specialist
- The interior designer
- The construction cost advisor
- The quality inspectors
  and so on

THE MAIN BUILDER
who commissions various companies to

- Demolish and remove old buildings
- Dig the basements
- Make the foundations
- Manufacture and erect the steelworks
- Mix and place the concrete
- Make and install the lifts (elevators)
- Buy and install the mechanicals and electricals
- Make and fix the windows
- Assemble and fix the cladding
- Supply and install the controls equipment
- Supply and install the fire protection
- Make and install the floors
- Make and install the ceilings
  and so on

Great skyscrapers of the world

NORTH AND SOUTH AMERICA

Home Insurance Company Building Chicago (1885)
Although only 10 storeys high this is generally accepted as the first skyscraper. It was the first building to make use of steel girder construction, and the outer wall did not carry the weight of the building.

Flatiron Building (formerly the Fuller Building) New York (1901–1903). This 21-storey, 87-metre (285 feet) building is an early example of a complete steel frame. Its heavy ornate stone façade was built top-down, an innovation in construction techniques.

Ingalls, Cincinnati (1903)
The first reinforced concrete skyscraper was designed by Elzner & Anderson with Henry N. Hooper as the structural engineer. Its 16 storeys are 64 metres (210 feet) high.

The Schlesinger-Meyer Store, Chicago (1904). This 12-storey building, still surprisingly modern in appearance, was designed by Louis Sullivan, who can be considered as the father of the skyscraper.

Woolworth Building, New York (1913). The headquarters of Woolworth Stores was built by the architect Cass Gilbert who also designed the New York Life Insurance Building (1928). It is 60 storeys, 242 metres (792 feet) high.

Chicago Tribune Tower, Chicago (1922)
This gothic style skyscraper, 141 metres (462 feet), was the subject of an architectural competition won by Raymond Hood who also designed the Daily News Building (1930) and McGraw Hill Building (1931) in New York.

Chrysler Building, New York (1930). Designed for Walter P Chrysler, founder of the automobile corporation, by William Van Alen. It is 77 storeys, 319 metres (1046 feet), and is decorated with symbolic designs from Chrysler's cars, and is capped with a stainless steel crown and spire – one of New York's most famous landmarks.

Empire State Building, New York (1931). For forty years this was the world's tallest building and is still probably its best-known skyscraper. Its entire structure, 102 storeys, 381 metres (1250 feet), was built in one year and forty-five days.

Waldorf Astoria Hotel, New York (1931). When it opened, this 500 bedroom, 47-storey hotel was the tallest in the world at 191 metres (625 feet).

Lake Shore Apartments, Chicago (1951)
These twin 26-storey apartment blocks built in structural steel are typical Mies van der Rohe skyscrapers. The structure allows the façade to be entirely glazed.

United Nations Building, New York (1952). This 39-storey, 154-metre (505-feet) building was designed by a consortium of the world's architects as the headquarters of the United Nations. Its steel frame was one of the last in which rivets were used.

Seagram Building, New York (1959). This dramatic tower with its external façade of bronze

28

columns and glass is 38 storeys, 160 metres (525 feet). It is perhaps the most famous building of the architect Mies van der Rohe, and is a classic example of the Modern Movement in architecture.

Marina City, Chicago (1962) These circular reinforced concrete, 65-storey towers, 179 metres (588 feet) high, house apartments each of which has a boat-mooring in the marina below.

Lake Point Towers, Chicago (1968). These reinforced concrete buildings, 70 storeys, 196 metres (645 feet) high are the tallest apartment buildings in the world.
John Hancock, Chicago (1968) The tallest, 343 metre (1127 feet), multi-use building in the world. Its 100 storeys are used for shopping, offices and apartments. The architects, Skidmore, Owings and Merrill, and their structural engineer partner, Fazlur Khan, developed the distinctive cross-braced structure on the facade so that the loads could be taken to enormous columns at the corners of the building.
One Shell Plaza, Houston (1969) 218 metres (715 feet) high, this is the tallest skyscraper built from lightweight concrete.
World Trade Center, New York (1973). These twin towers – 110 storeys, 412 metres (1350 feet) – designed by Minoru Yamasaki

(Japan), with Skille Robertson (USA) as structural engineers, are the tallest buildings in New York.
Transamerica Building, San Francisco (1972). Designed by William Pereira Partners this 48-storey, 257-metre (843-feet) building has a unique tapering shape.

John Hancock Tower, Boston (1973). This glass-clad skyscraper is steel framed. It has 60 storeys and rises to over 241 metres (790 feet). It was designed by I. M. Pei & Partners (USA).
Sears Tower, Chicago (1974) The world's tallest building, 110 storeys, 443 metres (1454 feet), designed by Skidmore, Owings and Merrill (USA). Its unusual plan consists of nine tubes each rising to a different height. The highest is capped with TV antennae which rise to 549 metres (1800 feet).
Water Tower Place, Chicago (1975). At 262 metres (859 feet) this is the tallest reinforced concrete skyscraper in the world.
Citicorp Center, New York (1977). This elegant white building with its distinctive sloping roof rises 59 storeys, 278 metres (914 feet) above Lexington Avenue.
Renaissance 1, Detroit (1977) This skyscraper is the tallest hotel in the United States, at 73 storeys 225 metres (739 feet). It has a reinforced concrete frame.
Texas Commerce Plaza, Houston (1981). 318 metres (1049 feet), 75 storeys, the tallest sky-

scraper built of a mixture of re-inforced concrete and structural steel.
333 Wacker Drive, Chicago (1983). Designed by Kohn Pedersen Fox of New York, this elegant, curved 37-storey, 144-metre (472 feet) skyscraper was a distinct change from the rectangular blocks of the 1970s.
American Telephones & Telegraph Building, New York (1984). This 198-metre (648-feet) building, though not tall by present standards, caused a sensation in the architectural world. The roof line, like a Chippendale highboy, was a complete break from the Modern Movement style and heralded a new approach to the form and decoration of skyscrapers.
Pittsburgh Plate Glass Building, Pittsburgh, Pennsylvania (1985) This 40-storey, 194-metre (635-feet) skyscraper is clad entirely in glass. Its highly sculptured and faceted elevation reflects the sky. It was designed by the American architects Philip Johnson and John Burgee, who also designed the Transco Tower in Houston, Texas.

Palacio Zarzur Kogan, Saõ Paolo, Brazil (1960) Brazil's tallest building, 170 metres (557 feet).
Hotel de Mexico, Mexico City, Mexico (1972). This 48-storey hotel, 175 metres (573 feet) high, is the tallest building in Mexico. It had to be designed to resist earthquake forces, and its stability was put to the test during the 1986 earthquake, when it remained unharmed.
Bank of Montreal, Toronto, Canada (1976). This steel-framed skyscraper is Canada's tallest, at 72 storeys, 290 metres (952 feet). It is used for offices, with a shopping complex at its base.
Parque Central Torre Oficinis, Caracas, Venezuela (1979) At 200 metres (656 feet), this 56-storey office block is the tallest building in South America, yet it is less than half the height of the Sears Tower in Chicago.

EUROPE

Centro Pirelli, Milan, Italy
(1958). Italy's tallest building, the headquarters of the Pirelli Tyre Company, is 128 metres (420 feet) high, and has 35 storeys of office floors.
Palace of Culture and Science, Warsaw, Poland (1955). The tallest building in Europe is styled rather like the American skyscrapers of the 1920s. Built of steel and reinforced concrete, it is 241 metres (790 feet) high.
Telecom Tower, London, UK (1965). Built both as an aerial tower and offices, the circular tower is 177 metres (580 feet) high.
Barbican Apartments, London, UK (1970). Three identical skyscrapers, designed by Chamberlain Powell and Bonn with the engineers Ove Arup & Partners, are the United Kingdom's tallest apartment buildings. Their 40 storeys rise 126 metres (412 feet) above a major arts centre.

Maine Montparnasse, Paris, France (1973)
At 64 storeys, this 229 metre (752 feet) office block is the tallest in France, yet it is still 70 metres (230 feet) lower than the Eiffel Tower. Built near the historic heart of Paris this building forced a change in the law forbidding the construction of skyscrapers close to the city centre.
National Westminster Bank, London, UK (1980)
At 182 metres (600 feet) and 52 storeys this is the tallest building in the United Kingdom. Designed by the British architect Richard Seifert, its structure is of structural steel and the central core was built by the slipform method.

AFRICA

Kenyatta Conference Centre, Nairobi, Kenya (1974)
The highest building in East Africa, at 105 metres (345 feet).
Standard Bank Centre, Johannesburg, South Africa (1970). 160 metres (525 feet) high, the floors of the building are hung from three huge beams spaced equally up the building. The architects were Hentrich & Petschnigg, with Ove Arup & Partners as engineers.
Carlton Centre, Johannesburg, South Africa (1973)
The tallest skyscraper on the African continent, this is a 50-storey, 220 metre (722 feet) concrete-framed office building. The architects were Skidmore, Owings and Merrill of the USA.

ASIA AND AUSTRALIA

MLC Centre, Sydney, Australia (1976). Sydney's tallest building at 240 metres (786 feet), 70 storeys, was designed by Harry Seidler with the Italian structural engineer Pier Luigi Nervi.
Sunshine Co., Tokyo, Japan (1978). This 60-storey block, 226 metres (742 feet), is the tallest building in Japan.
Hopewell Centre, Hong Kong (1981). This striking circular skyscraper of reinforced concrete rises 215 metres (707 feet). It was built on a steeply sloping site which presented very difficult foundation problems. The architects were Gordon Wu Associates, with Ove Arup & Partners as engineers.
Belmont Centre, Kuala Lumpur, Malaysia (1981)
This multi-use skyscraper is 193 metres (632 feet), 50 storeys high.
1 Queens Road Central, Hong Kong (1986). At 180 metres (590 feet), 51 storeys, though not as tall as the Hopewell Centre, this headquarters for the Hongkong and Shanghai Bank, designed by Foster Associates of London, is one of the island's most notable landmarks.
Rialto Building, Melbourne (1986). The tallest building in Australia, this skyscraper is 248 metres (794 feet) high.
Westin Stamford Hotel, Singapore (1986)
The tallest hotel in the world, this circular reinforced concrete skyscraper has 73 storeys and is 226 metres (742 feet) high.
Overseas Union Bank, Singapore (1986). The tallest skyscraper in Asia at 63 storeys, rising to 279 metres (919 feet). The architect was Kenzo Tange of Japan, and the structural engineers W. L. Meinhart & Partners of Australia. It has a composite steel and concrete frame.

The world's tallest buildings

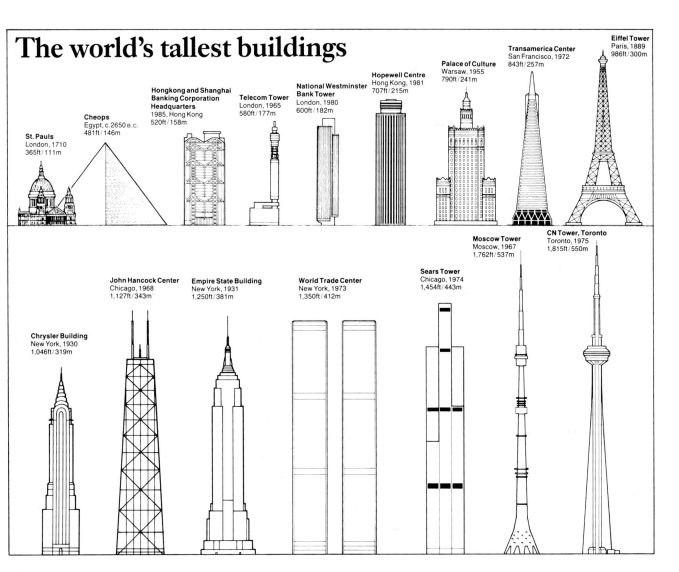

St. Pauls
London, 1710
365ft / 111m

Cheops
Egypt, c.2650 B.C.
481ft / 146m

Hongkong and Shanghai Banking Corporation Headquarters
1985, Hong Kong
520ft / 158m

Telecom Tower
London, 1965
580ft / 177m

National Westminster Bank Tower
London, 1980
600ft / 182m

Hopewell Centre
Hong Kong, 1981
707ft / 215m

Palace of Culture
Warsaw, 1955
790ft / 241m

Transamerica Center
San Francisco, 1972
843ft / 257m

Eiffel Tower
Paris, 1889
986ft / 300m

Chrysler Building
New York, 1930
1,046ft / 319m

John Hancock Center
Chicago, 1968
1,127ft / 343m

Empire State Building
New York, 1931
1,250ft / 381m

World Trade Center
New York, 1973
1,350ft / 412m

Sears Tower
Chicago, 1974
1,454ft / 443m

Moscow Tower
Moscow, 1967
1,762ft / 537m

CN Tower, Toronto
Toronto, 1975
1,815ft / 550m

Glossary

Cladding The outer skin of the building which is fixed after the frame has been built.

Column A vertical member in steel or concrete which takes the load of the building.

Compression A force which tends to reduce, or shorten, a material by pressure.

Façade The outer face of the building.

Footprint The plan-shape formed by the skyscraper on the ground.

Hangers Rods of steel, sometimes covered in concrete, which drop from the umbrella frame to hold up the floors.

Insulating jacket A cover round the steelwork which prevents the heat of the fire from reaching the steel.

Intelligent building A building in which a computer checks the environmental conditions and running of the machinery and automatically adjusts them to ensure that everything is working correctly.

Lightweight fibre A material, such as fibreglass, which does not burn. It is similar to the material which is used in the roof of a house to prevent heat escaping.

Pre-stressed concrete A development from reinforced concrete. Steel wires are stretched in the wet concrete so that when it hardens, the tension in the wire applies a compression to the concrete. Or steel rods are drawn through holes in the hardened concrete and then tensioned, putting the concrete in compression.

Porous aggregates Often made by melting natural materials, such as clay, and aerating them to form sponge-like stones.

Rivet A red hot lump of steel which is passed through holes in the steelwork and end-hammered to form a tight joint.

Ropes The steel cables which raise and lower lifts (elevators).

Self weight The weight of all the parts of the building, but not of the people or furniture in it.

Set-back From certain levels upwards a skyscraper reduces in plan area. This is known as set-back.

Umbrella frame A framework of beams which cantilever from the top of the building and from which the floors are hung.

Vermiculite Mica, a natural material, which, when heated to a high temperature, expands to form a sponge-like material.

Welding Joining up two pieces of adjacent steelwork by melting steel rods into the small gap between the pieces. The rods are melted by electric current or a gas flame.

Index

Acknowledgements

Threshold Books and the publishers gratefully acknowledge the help given by Ron Marsh.

Illustration credits
Photographs: Arup Associates page 20 (top); BET Plant Services 24 (top); British Lift Slab Ltd 16 (top and bottom); British Library MS Add 35313 f.34 9 (top left); British Telecom 24 (centre and bottom); Richard Bryant 2 (bottom); Ray Carpenter 5 (top left); Cement and Concrete Association UK 17 (top right); Chicago Tribune 5 (bottom right); Foster Associates 6 (top and bottom); Ian Lambot 26; George Eastman House/Lewis Hine 8 (top), 9 (bottom left), 12 (centre); John Hillelson Agency/Harold Sochurek 3; Hopewell Construction, Hong Kong 17 (centre, bottom left and bottom right); Timothy Hursley 5 (bottom centre); Edward Jacoby 15; Japan Information Centre 30; Kohn Pederson Fox, New York/Barbara Karant 21 Peter Mackertich 20 (bottom right), 28, 29 (left); Mexican Tourist Office 29 (right); John Mowlem 9 (top right); Novosti 30; Ove Arup & Partners 2 (top), 7 (top, centre and bottom), 8 (bottom), 10 (top and bottom), 11 (top, centre, bottom left and bottom right), 12 (bottom), 13 (top), 14 (bottom), 18, 19, 22, 23, 25, 30; William L Pereira Associates 29; Sue Prickett 5 (bottom left); Joseph E Seagram & Sons Inc./Ezra Stoller 14 (top); David Ward 20 (bottom left); ZEFA/H Winter 5 (top centre).

Diagrams and drawings: British Lift Slab Ltd/Ray Burrows 17 (top left); Ray Burrows 30 (bottom); Ray Carpenter 12 (top), 27; Grafton Books/*Multi Storey Buildings*, 2nd edition, by Hart, Henn and Sontag 13 (bottom)

Picture research: Pat Mandel.

First published in 1987
by Faber and Faber Limited,
3 Queen Square, London WC1N 3AU
Typeset by August Filmsetting, Haydock, St. Helens

Printed and bound in Italy by New Interlitho, Milan
All rights reserved
© Threshold Books Limited, 1987

The How It Is Made series was conceived, designed, and produced
by Threshold Books Limited,
661 Fulham Road, London SW6 5PZ

General Editor: Barbara Cooper

British Library Cataloguing in Publication Data

Michael, Duncan
  Skyscrapers.—(How it is made)
  1. Skyscrapers—Juvenile literature
  I. Title   II. Series
  721′.042   NA6230
  ISBN 0–571–14730–5